345.7)
MAR
2008

Privacy Rights and
The Patriot Act

Essential Viewpoints

PRIVACY RIGHTS AND

THE PATRIOT ACT

BY HAROLD MARCOVITZ

Content Consultant
Charles Lee Mudd Jr., Adjunct Faculty
John Marshall Law School

ABDO
Publishing Company

CREDITS

Published by ABDO Publishing Company, 8000 West 78th Street, Edina, Minnesota 55439. Copyright © 2008 by Abdo Consulting Group, Inc. International copyrights reserved in all countries. No part of this book may be reproduced in any form without written permission from the publisher. The Essential Library™ is a trademark and logo of ABDO Publishing Company.

Printed in the United States

Editor: Patricia Stockland
Copy Editor: Paula Lewis
Interior Design and Production: Emily Love
Cover Design: Emily Love

Library of Congress Cataloging-in-Publication Data
Marcovitz, Harold.
  Privacy rights and the Patriot Act / Harold Marcovitz.
    p. cm. — (Essential viewpoints)
  Includes bibliographical references and index.
  ISBN 978-1-60453-059-9
  1. United States. Uniting and Strengthening America by Providing Appropriate Tools Required to Intercept and Obstruct Terrorism (USA PATRIOT ACT) Act of 2001—Juvenile literature. 2. Terrorism—United States—Prevention—Juvenile literature. 3. Privacy, Right of—United States—Juvenile literature. 4. Civil rights—United States—Juvenile literature. 5. Law enforcement—United States—Juvenile literature. I. Title.

  KF9430.M37 2008
  345.73'02—dc22
                                    2007031919

TABLE OF CONTENTS

Massive damage and tributes in New York City, New York, after the 2001 terrorist attacks

THE CASE OF JOHN DOE

*I*n the weeks following the September 11, 2001, terrorist attacks, the U.S. Congress drafted a law that would help the Federal Bureau of Investigation (FBI) and other law enforcement agencies gather information on suspected terrorists.

The new law, the USA Patriot Act, was signed by the president on October 26—just 45 days after the attacks.

Members of Congress, fearful that terrorists were planning more attacks against U.S. citizens, voted in favor of the law by an overwhelming majority and with little debate. The act passed the House by a vote of 357 to 66. In the Senate, only one senator in the 100-member body voted against the Patriot Act. Clearly, members of Congress aimed to ensure that no terrorist would strike again on U.S. soil. When he signed the law, President Bush said, "This government will enforce this law with all the urgency of a nation at war."[1]

The Patriot Act contained many provisions that could serve as important tools in locating terrorists. It permits the arrest and detention of immigrants for up to a week before charges must be filed. The U.S. Constitution had allowed those arrested to quickly learn the

Lone Voice of Dissent

The lone member of the U.S. Senate to vote against the Patriot Act was Democrat Russell Feingold of Wisconsin. On October 25, 2001, Feingold took the Senate floor to speak against the passage of the Patriot Act. He said, "It is one thing to shortcut the legislative process in order to get federal financial aid to the cities hit by terrorism. We did that, and no one complained that we moved too quickly. It is quite another to press for the enactment of sweeping new powers for law enforcement that directly affect the civil liberties of the American people without due deliberation by the people's elected representatives."[2]

charges filed against them. The Patriot Act provided more time for investigators to question the suspects before they had to be charged or let go. The Patriot Act also made it easier for different federal agencies to share information with one another about suspected terrorist plots.

Acts of Terror on U.S. Soil

The attacks of September 11, 2001, were committed by radical Islamic fundamentalists who hijacked two airliners and crashed them into the Twin Towers of the World Trade Center in New York. Two other planes were also hijacked. One crashed into the Pentagon in Washington, D.C., while the other crashed in rural Pennsylvania after passengers overpowered the hijackers. Investigators believe the plane was headed for the White House. In all, more than 3,000 people lost their lives.

The September 11 attacks are regarded as the most horrific acts of terrorism ever committed on U.S. soil, but there have been others. They include:

- The 1995 bombing of the Alfred P. Murrah Federal Building in Oklahoma City, Oklahoma, which killed 168 people. The anti-government terrorist Timothy McVeigh was convicted and executed in 2001.
- In 1993, Islamic terrorists exploded a bomb in the parking garage of the World Trade Center, killing six people.
- In 1975, four people were killed when a group seeking independence for Puerto Rico set off a bomb in Fraunces Tavern in New York.
- In 1973, Marcus Foster, the superintendent of schools of Oakland, California, was murdered by the Symbionese Liberation Army.

A Change in Checks and Balances

The Patriot Act included a number of provisions that alarmed civil libertarians—individuals and members of groups who oppose government intrusion into the lives of citizens. The act's provisions enabled federal agents to gain easy access to private records. These records included financial information maintained by banks, health records kept by hospitals and physicians, and e-mail usage records kept by Internet service providers. Under the Patriot Act, even libraries would be required to turn over the records of books that cardholders had checked out. Federal officials argued that such records could provide clues to the intentions of a terrorist.

In the past, those records were always available to the FBI as well as local police departments. However, to obtain the records, the police had to convince a judge to issue an order known as a warrant. In many cases, the person under investigation had the right to go to court to fight the issuance of the warrant. Under the Patriot Act,

Fear of Totalitarianism

Under the Patriot Act, certain searches can be conducted without approval of a judge. Oakland, California, city attorney John A. Russo, former director of the National League of Cities, believes that a search without a judge's approval is the type of drastic measure that leaders of totalitarian governments have used to silence their enemies.

He said, "Were a totalitarian government to be imposed on us, its inception would look strikingly like these provisions. History teaches us that such evils almost always begin justified by concerns for public safety and amid general panic. Without judicial safeguards, federal agents could abuse their newly authorized tools in situations neither Congress nor the American people contemplated."[3]

the FBI no longer has to seek a warrant from a judge. The agent could obtain the information by serving the bank, hospital, or library with a National Security Letter. The person served with a National Security Letter is required by law to comply immediately and may not reveal to others that he or she had received such a letter. Also, the person under investigation would never learn about the issuance of the letter and have no way of blocking it in court.

Government Database

Through the issuance of National Security Letters, the FBI has created a database that contains more than 560 million separate records. Civil libertarians say it is clear the database contains information on Americans who have no ties to terrorism.

Potential for Abuse

Windsor, Connecticut, hardly seems like a place where a terrorist would plan a deadly strike against U.S. citizens. The town of just 29,000 people features no towering skyscrapers and no large military bases, both of which are regarded as likely terrorist targets. And yet, in July 2005, an FBI agent served a library official in Windsor with a National Security Letter, authorizing the release of records that the agent believed could help thwart a terror plot.

The agent had received an anonymous e-mail suggesting that a terrorist attack was being planned. The FBI traced the source of the e-mail to a public library computer in Connecticut and demanded that the library official turn over Internet records for all users of the library. Libraries guard the privacy of their members closely. Librarians have long resisted efforts by the government and others to reveal lists of members, readership habits, and other information maintained in their records.

Instead of immediately complying, the library official enlisted the American Civil Liberties Union (ACLU) to sue the federal government on the grounds that certain provisions of the Patriot Act violate people's rights to privacy. The ACLU is the leading

First Conviction

The first defendant arrested and convicted on evidence gathered under the Patriot Act was Mohamed Hussein, a Somali immigrant. Hussein allegedly funneled money to the al-Qaeda terrorist network, the organization responsible for the September 11, 2001, attacks.

Federal agents initiated an investigation of Hussein in October 2001. Hussein, whose bank records were seized by the FBI, was arrested and charged with running an unlicensed money-wiring business. He was convicted in 2002 and sentenced to 18 months in prison.

George Christian, left, and the other three members of the Library Connection who were issued National Security Letters

advocacy group in the United States for defending citizens who oppose actions by the government that they believe go beyond the law.

In the lawsuit filed by the ACLU, the library official was identified as "John Doe" because the Patriot Act prohibits the public identification of the recipient of a National Security Letter. In this case, the ACLU argued that recipients of National Security Letters should be allowed to identify themselves and contest the letters in court.

The ACLU also argued that there were few checks
and balances pertaining to the Patriot Act. If the FBI
abused its powers, librarians and others could not
report the misdeeds.

The judge agreed with the ACLU's position and
ruled that the portion of the Patriot Act forcing
recipients of National Security Letters to remain
silent was unconstitutional. In her legal opinion,
Judge Hall wrote,

> *The potential for abuse is written into the statute; the very
> people who might have information regarding investigative
> abuses and overreaching are preemptively prevented from
> sharing that information with the public.*[4]

Maintaining a Free Society

Eventually, it was revealed that John Doe was
not one librarian but four employees of Library
Connection. This nonprofit company based in
Windsor coordinates Internet services for 27
Connecticut libraries. George Christian, the
executive director of Library Connection, was one
of the recipients of the National Security Letter. In
2007, Christian testified before a U.S. Senate panel
probing abuses of the Patriot Act,

The "Connecticut Four" continue to feel strongly that libraries were and should remain pillars of democracy, institutions where citizens could come to explore their concerns, confident that they could find information on all sides of controversial issues and confident that their explorations would remain personal and private. For example, a woman looking for information on divorce or breast cancer does not want those concerns known to anyone else; a student who wants to study about the Qur'an shouldn't have to wonder if the government is second-guessing why he is interested in this topic; a business owner curious about markets for his products or services in the Middle East should not have to worry that by researching these markets at the public library he will arouse FBI suspicions. As one of my fellow John Does put it, "Spying on people in the library is like spying on them in the voting booth."[5]

The judge in the John Doe case ruled that the gag order violated the First and Fourth Amendments.

The Heart of the Controversy

In 2007, the FBI disclosed that its agents had served as many as 143,074 National Security Letters (NSLs) since the Patriot Act was signed into law in October 2001. That number does not include approximately 2,000 letters that were issued without proper authorization. Before 2001, the letters had to go through a tougher process before being issued. In 2000, only 8,500 letters were issued. NSLs have been available since 1978. The FBI originally used the letters to find Soviet spies. The Patriot Act made the letters more available and their use less restricted.

Those in favor of the Patriot Act note that government agencies now have more freedom and flexibility in protecting the nation by uncovering terrorist actions. Certainly, much of the information gathered by agents has been used to uncover terror plots and build cases against suspects.

Critics argue that a large amount of the information gathered with the help of the Patriot Act has delved into the private lives of individuals with no connection to terrorism. For example, after the FBI lost the John Doe case, the agency

Violated Amendments

Some people question whether the Patriot Act violates certain rights of citizens. These rights include those guaranteed by the First and Fourth Amendments. The First Amendment ensures citizens the right to criticize the government by exercising freedom of speech and freedom of the press. The Fourth Amendment protects citizens against searches conducted without warrants.

Phantoms of Lost Liberty

Former U.S. Attorney General John Ashcroft oversaw the drafting of the Patriot Act (actually named H. R. 3162). From the time the measure became law until he left office in 2005, Ashcroft was a steadfast defender of the Patriot Act, leveling harsh criticism at opponents who suggested the laws trampled on civil liberties. He said, "To those who scare peace-loving people with phantoms of lost liberty, my message is this: Your tactics only aid terrorists—for they erode our national unity and diminish our resolve. They give ammunition to America's enemies, and pause to America's friends. They encourage people of good will to remain silent in the face of evil."[6]

disclosed that its investigation into the Connecticut terror plot revealed that the original e-mail threat was a hoax. The John Doe case illustrates that in times of crisis, some citizens, as well as government leaders, believe it is necessary to sacrifice certain rights in the interest of protecting human lives and national security. Others believe that maintaining such rights as freedom of speech and the right to privacy is what keeps the United States a free society.

*President George W. Bush raises a U.S. flag during rescue efforts after the
2001 terrorist attacks.*

George W. Bush, seated, *signing the Patriot Act in 2001*

SWIFT RESPONSE
TO A CRISIS

*D*uring the nine days after the September 11, 2001, attacks, the Justice Department began circulating proposals for increased powers for law enforcement. The 342-page document submitted to Congress was named the Uniting and

Strengthening America by Providing Appropriate Tools Required to Intercept and Obstruct Terrorism Act of 2001 or, for short, the USA PATRIOT Act. The members of Congress made few changes to the document. Some members of Congress worried that the act trampled too heavily on civil liberties—particularly the right to privacy. But given the demand that terrorist cells be exposed, the voices of opposition to the Patriot Act were few. One of the few voices of dissent was Georgetown University law professor David Cole, who said:

> [In] World War II we interned 110,000 Japanese Americans solely for their ethnic ancestry. [In] World War I we locked up people for speaking out against the war ... So we've made very serious mistakes in the past. All of those are now recognized as mistakes. But at the time, of course, they seemed quite reasonable, quite necessary, to a broad segment of the American public.[1]

"Fear Is Unfounded"

Former U.S. Assistant Attorney General Viet Dinh, author of the Patriot Act, said opponents have unfairly characterized the law's effect on civil liberties. He stated, "I ... recognize that the act has been mischaracterized and misunderstood and has engendered a lot of well-meaning and genuine fear, even if that fear is unfounded. The issue is not one of substance but one of perception. But perception is also very important because we do not want the people, however many of them, to fear the government when that fear is unfounded."[2]

Patriot Act Author
Viet Dinh

Viet Dinh served in the U.S. Justice Department from 2001 to 2003. As a boy, Dinh escaped from communist Vietnam. After a harrowing journey in a leaky boat, Dinh and his family made it to Malaysia. Eventually, the Dinhs immigrated to the United States, where they found work as fruit pickers in Oregon and California.

Dinh took advantage of his opportunities in the United States and graduated from Harvard Law School. Now a professor at Georgetown School of Law in Washington, D.C., Dinh is regarded as a future candidate for the U.S. Supreme Court. If selected, he would be the first Asian American to sit on the nation's highest court.

Viet Dinh, an assistant attorney general in the Justice Department, was the chief architect of the Patriot Act. Dinh pointed out that the Patriot Act did receive congressional oversight—Congress reviewed the document for six weeks before legislators gave the new law their overwhelming approval. He acknowledged that it is rare for Congress to act so quickly, but lawmakers realized the importance of their mission—to prevent future terror plots and protect American lives. Professor David Cole commented on the speed at which the act was passed,

> There is undoubtedly a balance to be struck between liberty and security, but there are also several reasons to be cautious about too readily sacrificing liberty in the name of security. First, as a historical

Viet Dinh

matter, we have often overreacted in times of crisis. ... In hindsight, these responses are generally viewed as shameful excesses; but in their day, they were considered reasonable and necessary.[3]

Most Americans, as well as President Bush, however, agreed with Dinh. President Bush insisted that the Justice Department would respect the civil rights of law-abiding U.S. citizens when investigating terror plots. During a White House ceremony on the day he signed the Patriot Act, Bush said,

> *One thing is certain: These terrorists must be pursued; they must be defeated; and they must be brought to justice. And that is the purpose of this legislation. ... The men and women of our intelligence and law enforcement agencies ... deserve our full support and every means of help that we can provide.*[4]

CONTROVERSIAL PROVISIONS

The Patriot Act's original version included provisions that caused little controversy. There are other provisions, however, that many people feel compromise civil liberties. These controversial provisions include:

❖ Legalizing sneak-and-peek searches. This enables federal agents to search a private home

---

Former Rules for National Security Letters

Under the provisions of the Patriot Act passed in 2001, a federal agent had to demonstrate to a higher-ranking authority that the records he or she was seeking with a National Security Letter were "relevant" to an investigation that was probing the activities of international terrorist cells or foreign agents. Prior to the Patriot Act, the test was much higher. Before a National Security Letter could be issued, the agent had to prove a specific record or document could play a significant role in uncovering the activities of the suspects.

without informing the resident of a warrant.

❖ Enabling prosecutors to obtain search warrants that can be served anywhere in the country. Prior to the Patriot Act, a warrant could be served only in the immediate region in which it was obtained. Now, for example, a judge in New Jersey can issue a warrant that can be served in California.

❖ Relaxing the rules under which wiretap warrants can be obtained from the Foreign Intelligence Surveillance Court. This makes the wiretaps available for criminal investigations. Prior to the Patriot Act, listening devices were solely limited to intelligence-gathering functions.

Hunting Communists at the Library

One of the reasons librarians guard the identities of their members so closely is because of a 1950s-era initiative by the federal government known as the Library Awareness Program. As part of the program, FBI agents demanded to know whether library members with European-sounding names had checked out scientific books. The FBI suspected that communist spies were culling through American libraries for clues on how to build nuclear weapons. Once the program was revealed, many state governments passed "freedom to read" laws, protecting the identities of library members and the lists of books they have checked out.

❖ Using roving wiretaps. This permits
agents to eavesdrop on any phone or other
communication device a suspect might use. In
the past, police had to obtain a separate warrant
for each device.

❖ Allowing federal agents to search through
private records by obtaining National Security
Letters from a mid-level FBI official. Prior to
the Patriot Act, the threshold for obtaining the
letters was much higher.

❖ Expanding search warrants to Internet use.
Agents can monitor e-mail and track visits to
Web sites.

Some of these investigative techniques have been
employed in the past, but they were conducted
under strict oversight by a judge who was charged
with ensuring that the constitutional rights of the
suspects were not violated. Under the Patriot Act,
investigations can be conducted with far less judicial
oversight. Laura Murphy, national lobbying director
of the ACLU, said,

*It goes beyond fighting terrorism. It makes fundamental
changes in criminal procedure. The police can now come into*

your home, download information off of your computer, go
through your personal possessions, and you'll never know
that they were there.[5]

Protecting Americans' Privacy

Throughout history, Congress has passed numerous acts to further ensure U.S. citizens' right to privacy. In 1974, Congress passed the Privacy Act, which protected many of the records the government keeps on citizens from disclosure. In 1988, the Privacy Act guarantees were extended to

Habeas Corpus

The Patriot Act is not the first example of the government acting swiftly in a time of crisis. During the Civil War, President Abraham Lincoln suspended habeas corpus. Habeas corpus is a Latin term that means, "You ought to have the person." If a judge issues a writ of habeas corpus, a prosecutor is required to produce the prisoner in court so that he or she may hear the charges and stand trial. If the prosecutor lacks evidence to make a case against the prisoner, the judge can order the prisoner's release.

When Abraham Lincoln suspended habeas corpus during the Civil War, he refused to produce the prisoners in the civilian courts that had issued the writs. Instead, he had the prisoners tried in military courts, contending that they were traitors to the Union. Yale University law professor Akhil Reed Amar said most of the prisoners jailed by Lincoln were residents of Maryland—including the mayor of Baltimore. Maryland was a Confederate-leaning state that posed a danger to the Union because it surrounds Washington, D.C., the nation's capital. Virginia, which borders Washington across the Potomac River, had seceded from the Union. There was a real risk of the White House being captured.

computerized records as well. Health records, tax information, and even a student's school records are protected under various acts.

In the past, these records and other personal documents kept by the government could be obtained by federal agents pursuing criminal investigations—as long as they obtained a warrant by proving to a judge that the records were vital to preventing or solving a crime. However, the Patriot Act relaxes many of the constraints placed on the procurement of the records, making them much easier for a federal law enforcement officer to obtain. Even a student's school records can be seized under the Patriot Act and used to build a criminal case. ⌐

Some people concerned with their privacy rights have started petitions
against the Patriot Act.

Attorney Neal Sonnet addresses delegates of the American Bar Association regarding his task force findings on domestic spying.

TWO SIDES
OF THE DEBATE

The Patriot Act has sparked heated debate in American society. On one side of the debate are those, including the National League of Cities, who believe the Patriot Act is vital to

protecting Americans from terrorism. On the
other side of the debate are those who believe the
government has no business in the private affairs
of citizens. Those who are against the Patriot Act
include liberal organizations such as the ACLU
and conservative groups such as the American
Conservative Union. In addition, more than 400
city councils, as well as the legislatures of seven
states, passed resolutions calling for either the repeal
of the act or a rollback of some of its anti-privacy
provisions.

Since the law was first enacted, polls have
continually indicated that most citizens are willing
to sacrifice some of their personal liberties in the
interest of identifying terrorists and preventing
terrorist acts. Other Americans believe the
government has gone too far.

The surveillance techniques authorized by the
Patriot Act have sparked the most debate. The
Patriot Act gives the FBI permission to employ
roving wiretaps, engage in domestic spying, monitor
e-mail, and participate in sneak-and-peek searches.
Civil libertarians believe these surveillance methods
could lead to abuses, such as targeting legitimate
public advocacy groups through domestic spying.

Opposition in North Pole, Alaska

One of the more than 400 American cities that passed a resolution opposing the Patriot Act was North Pole, Alaska. The community of approximately 1,500 people is located just south of the city of Fairbanks in central Alaska. In 2003, the city council unanimously passed a resolution that stated, "The North Pole City Council requests members of the U.S. Congress to immediately re-examine the U.S. Patriot Act that it passed in October 2001, amending any portion of it that infringes upon civil rights of U.S. citizens."[1]

SHOULD ROVING WIRETAPS BE PERMITTED?

Prior to the Patriot Act, the FBI had to obtain separate warrants for each communication device that it wanted to tap into. The process could take several days to prepare the warrant, schedule a hearing before a judge, and install the eavesdropping equipment. By then, the terrorist may have made his communications and switched devices—meaning the FBI would need to start over by requesting a new warrant. The Patriot Act permits a judge to issue a blanket warrant for every device that a suspected terrorist is likely to use, including phones and pagers.

IN FAVOR: THE PATRIOT ACT MODERNIZES LAW ENFORCEMENT

Supporters argue that the Patriot Act's roving wiretap provision has helped bring law enforcement into the twenty-first century, particularly in its

expansion of the use of electronic surveillance.
Terrorists frequently make use of several phones,
particularly cell phones. Now, the roving wiretap
provision of the Patriot Act permits a single warrant
to follow the terrorist from phone to phone.

Opposed: The Patriot Act Invades Privacy Rights

Opponents believe the wiretap provision of the
law goes too far. If a suspected terrorist visits a friend
in that person's home, the Patriot Act gives the FBI
authority to tap the friend's phone as well. The
visit may have been entirely social, and the alleged
terrorist's friend may have no connection to any
plot. But the FBI can argue that the suspect used his
friend's phone to plan a terrorist strike and use the
roving wiretap provision to listen in on an innocent
person's phone calls.

Should the FBI Spy on Domestic Groups?

The FBI's power to investigate domestic
organizations has been widely cut since the 1960s.
During that time, the agency was believed to have
abused its powers by launching investigations of anti-
Vietnam War activists, student leaders, civil rights

COINTELPRO

During the twentieth century, many Americans feared communism. Starting in the 1950s, undercover agents infiltrated communist organizations. The agents created discord, spread rumors and lies, and encouraged members to reveal secrets. Their efforts helped shut down the communist movement in the United States.

In the 1960s, agents used similar tactics against civil rights groups and student organizations protesting the Vietnam War. J. Edgar Hoover, the longtime director of the FBI, regarded these groups as dangerous. When secret documents chronicling the abuses of power by the FBI were leaked to journalists in 1971, COINTELPRO was quickly shut down.

leaders, and others who opposed the government. This program of domestic spying was called COINTELPRO, which stood for Counterintelligence Program.

The FBI kept Dr. Martin Luther King Jr., one of the nation's most important civil rights leaders, under surveillance for several years. Government officials felt King and others could stir up passions and incite rioting and other violence. But the FBI violated these citizens' civil rights by keeping them under observation.

The Justice Department implemented constraints on the FBI to ensure that it does not engage in domestic spying. One of those constraints prohibited the FBI from using evidence in a criminal court that it had gathered through a wiretap from the Foreign Intelligence Surveillance Court. Instead, the information could be used only for intelligence purposes.

Lawmakers also specified that the warrants could not be used to build criminal cases but only to gather intelligence that would assist the government in its relations with foreign powers. The FBI could use wiretaps to build a criminal case only if it already had probable cause to believe the suspected group or its members had perpetrated an offense or were planning to commit a crime. In those cases, the FBI could not obtain its warrant for a wiretap from the Foreign Intelligence Surveillance Court. The agency had to obtain a warrant from a federal court operating in a public courtroom.

Under previous legal constraints, the FBI's investigative powers were limited, and the terrorist threat continued to grow. Drug cartels, organized crime families, and similar groups represented security threats that remained largely unchecked. With the passing of the Patriot Act, the FBI would be able to act more extensively against these groups. But would the extension of investigative power be used against groups other than criminals and terrorists?

Potential for Abuse of Power?

Opponents suggest the Patriot Act is too broad and could be used to characterize political activists such as Greenpeace and the Environmental Liberation Front as terrorist groups. Occasionally, such organizations have bent the law and engaged in nonviolent civil disobedience to protest antienvironmental measures or corporations. Most U.S. civil rights groups would hardly be characterized as terrorist organizations, yet the FBI could make use of provisions in the Patriot Act to spy on them. Civil libertarians suggest that under the Patriot Act, federal agents could use their authority to obtain records on their leaders and use them to develop criminal cases.

Civil libertarians contend that federal agents could also use the Foreign Intelligence Surveillance Court to seek evidence against activist groups. Dana Lesemann, a former staff attorney for the Foreign Intelligence Surveillance Court, said she was frequently pressured by FBI agents to prepare warrants that did not target suspected foreign spies:

> You'd have an FBI agent screaming, "I need this warrant and I need it now." He's screaming, "People will die unless you go to court." Or an agent would say, "This is a bad person, we need to move on this," and I'd say, "Yes, this is a bad person, but there's no 'foreign power' here.[2]

In Favor: The FBI Should Monitor Internet Use

The Patriot Act has given federal agents greater authority in obtaining records of an individual's Internet use, including e-mail. Advocates argue that the previous laws governing investigations of terrorists and other suspects were written before the Internet became an important mode of communication. As such, agents had little authority to look into Internet records, yet terrorists could easily make plans and swap information using e-mail.

With the Patriot Act, the FBI can determine whether suspects visit Web sites known to promote violence against Americans. When President Bush signed the Patriot Act, he said,

> We're dealing with terrorists who operate by highly sophisticated methods and technologies, some of which were not even available when our existing laws were written. The bill before me takes account of the new realities and dangers posed by modern terrorists. It will help law enforcement to identify, to dismantle, to disrupt, and to punish terrorists before they strike.[3]

Opposed: The Law Allows for Information Mining

Opponents argue that the Patriot Act allows the FBI to mine information from computers, where people maintain records of their health, finances, and other personal details. Also, under the authority of the Patriot Act, the FBI can tell whether an individual visits an anti-American Web site—even though that individual may have no ill intentions toward the United States but is simply interested in what the site has to say.

Pen/Traps and Carnivore

In the days of rotary telephones, police could obtain telephone numbers of suspects by using a device known as a pen register. The pen register did not record the telephone call, just the number being dialed. A similar instrument, known as a trap, recorded numbers received by a phone.

Even though the conversations were not recorded, this information could prove to be important. It helped investigators discover who the suspects called as well as who called the suspects. Together, these techniques for gathering evidence are known as pen/traps.

The Patriot Act gives the FBI the authority to extend this style of investigation to the Internet. Agents can obtain e-mail addresses that terror suspects collect in their Internet service accounts. To collect e-mail addresses, the FBI developed a software program known as Carnivore. In addition to collecting e-mail addresses, Carnivore can also assess the person's Web surfing habits.

"Instead of a finely tuned instrument to pick up what was needed, it just scooped up everything," said David McClure, president of the U.S. Internet Industry Association based in Alexandria, Virginia.[4] In 2005, the FBI shelved Carnivore after obtaining more sophisticated software for culling through e-mail.

Opponents argue that the
Patriot Act does not specifically
permit federal agents to read
e-mail. It only allows agents to
obtain the e-mail addresses of
the suspect's correspondents.
However, because the e-mail's
content is automatically attached
to the addresses, critics suggest
there is little to prevent the agent
from viewing the entire e-mail.
Opponents question whether
agents can be trusted to delete the
messages without reading them.

IN FAVOR: SNEAK-AND-PEEK IS LEGAL

Law enforcement agencies
always have had the right to search
a suspect's home, business, automobile, or other
property. However, police first had to obtain a
search warrant from a judge. Next, the warrant had
to be served and posted as the search was conducted.
Before searching the property, police were required
to knock and announce their search. This provision

**The Case against
Sami al-Arian**

Since the 1990s, al-Arian,
a former computer science professor at the University of South Florida,
has been a leader of the
Islamic Committee for
Palestine, a group the
FBI suspected was raising
money for terrorists. Under the Patriot Act, the FBI
launched an investigation
of the group. In 2003,
the FBI produced some
20,000 hours of wiretap
records against al-Arian
and charged him with
raising money for terrorists. In 2006, he pleaded
guilty to one count of
conspiracy and was sentenced to 57 months in
prison, the maximum under a plea of guilty. Under
the plea agreement, he
will be deported after his
release from jail.

of the law guaranteed the suspect the right to know about the search, retain an attorney, and seek available legal remedies. In a sneak-and-peek search, the agents still have to obtain a warrant, but they are not required to tell the suspect of its existence until after the search.

Proponents of the Patriot Act regard sneak-and-peek as a valuable tool to combat terrorism. They argue that if the suspect has prior knowledge that a search will occur, they could hide or destroy evidence and flee.

Opposed: Sneak-and-Peek Is an Invasion of Privacy

Sneak-and-peek has long been opposed by civil libertarians, who regard it as an intrusion on a person's privacy. They argue that under a sneak-and-peek order, there is nothing to prevent a federal agent from entering somcone's house, going through personal possessions, downloading data from a computer, and leaving with details about that person's private life. Ultimately, civil libertarians argue, the federal agent will be in possession of private information on a person who may have no connection to a terror plot. ⌐

Attorney General John Ashcroft discussing progress in a terror cell case

MAKING OUR COMMUNITY SAFE

George W. Bush speaks about the Patriot Act at the Ohio State Highway Patrol Academy in Columbus, Ohio.

How the Patriot Act Benefits Law Enforcement

The Patriot Act has led to the arrests and convictions of many people who were planning terrorist acts against the United States and its allies. In 2005, President Bush said the Patriot

Act had been employed to prosecute more than 400 defendants. Some independent studies have disputed that number.

One year later, when Bush signed legislation reauthorizing the Patriot Act, he pointed out that the law had been used to break up terror cells in Ohio, New York, Oregon, and Virginia. He also mentioned that individual terrorists and their supporters had been prosecuted in California, Texas, New Jersey, Illinois, Washington, and North Carolina. "The Patriot Act is vital to the war on terror and defending our citizens against a ruthless enemy," Bush stated during the signing ceremony.[1]

The Wall

The Patriot Act authorizes federal agents to use the Foreign Intelligence Surveillance Court to obtain evidence that can be used in criminal cases. This breaks down what law enforcement officials

Disrupting Terror Threats

According to the U.S. Justice Department, by 2005, a total of 401 suspects had been arrested under the Patriot Act. Of that number, 212 pleaded guilty or were convicted.

Other statistics released by the Justice Department included:

- Forty organizations with links to terrorist groups in the United States or other countries have been identified.
- More than 500 aliens with links to terror cells have been deported to their home countries.
- A total of 113 suspects have been charged with raising money for terror plots; 57 have been convicted.

have called the "wall." This invisible barrier kept intelligence agents from sharing information with law enforcement officers who were investigating criminals.

The wall was created by Congress to ensure that the FBI and other law enforcement agencies did not engage in domestic spying. By creating the Foreign Intelligence Surveillance Court, Congress recognized that intelligence gathering and law enforcement are two separate groups, each with its own individual tasks and goals.

The job of the law enforcement, or criminal investigations, officer is to gather evidence on a criminal that can be used in court. The officer uses the evidence to arrest and convict the suspect. In contrast, the job of the intelligence agent is to learn what a foreign government is doing. That information may

Internet Predators and the Patriot Act

In 2002, 13-year-old Alicia Kozakiewicz left her home in Pittsburgh, Pennsylvania, to join a man she had met in an Internet chat room. The man, Scott Tyree, kidnapped the girl and imprisoned her in his home in Herndon, Virginia. A Florida man who corresponded with Tyree on the Internet heard about the case and suspected Tyree was the perpetrator. He contacted the FBI and provided agents with Tyree's e-mail address. Using the Patriot Act, FBI agents obtained Tyree's name and address from his Internet service provider. The agents located the girl three days after her abduction. Tyree was arrested, convicted, and sentenced to nearly 20 years in prison.

be used by the National Security Agency, the Central Intelligence Agency (CIA), or the State Department to help the president and his or her administration formulate foreign policy.

PRIME SUSPECT

At no time was the wall more evident than in the months leading up to the terrorist attacks of September 11, 2001. By the summer of 2001, the CIA had developed intelligence suggesting al-Qaeda was planning a major attack in the United States. FBI intelligence agents started culling through records of known al-Qaeda members. Nineteen days before the attacks, an intelligence agent recognized Khalid al-Midhar, a Saudi man, in a photo taken in Malaysia. A quick check of passport records indicated that al-Midhar had entered the United States legally in July. The intelligence agent recommended that al-Midhar be located and picked up for questioning. However, since an intelligence agent, rather than a criminal investigations officer, made the recommendation, the FBI placed far less priority on locating al-Midhar. The request to locate al-Midhar was forwarded to other intelligence agents—not to the criminal investigations staff.

Months after al-Midhar surfaced as a person of interest to the FBI, he boarded a plane in Washington, D.C., on September 11, 2001, and crashed it into the Pentagon, killing nearly 200 victims. Had the intelligence staff been able to share information with the criminal investigations staff,

it may have been possible to have prevented al-Midhar from carrying out his terrorist attack.

With the Patriot Act, which allows the sharing of information between the agencies, authorities may be better equipped to prevent similar attacks in the future. President Bush observed,

> You hear the talk about the walls that separate certain aspects of government; they have been removed by the Patriot Act. And now, law enforcement and intelligence communities are working together to share information to better prevent an attack on America. [2]

Using the Patriot Act against Drug Dealers

Federal agents in Florida used the Patriot Act to smash a ring of Colombian drug dealers. Wiretapping the phones of the conspirators had proven difficult because the suspects frequently changed cell phones. At one point, the agents had tapped more than 20 separate phone lines without producing evidence against the ring. In 2005, the agents obtained a warrant for a roving wiretap, which is permitted under the Patriot Act. The suspects were ultimately arrested and convicted of distributing cocaine.

José Padilla, center, is escorted by federal marshals.

DIRTY BOMBS

Within days of the enactment of the Patriot Act, the wall that had separated intelligence gathering from criminal investigations had been broken. Proponents of the Patriot Act contended that the arrest of José Padilla, an American citizen, proved the wall had not only been broken—it was smashed into rubble.

Padilla was believed to have been planning to detonate a "dirty bomb" on a U.S. city. A dirty bomb contains radioactive materials or chemical or biological substances. When a dirty bomb explodes, it releases its poisonous contents into the atmosphere, potentially killing dozens or even hundreds of people.

In May 2002, Padilla was arrested at O'Hare International Airport in Chicago, Illinois. He had just returned from a visit to several Middle Eastern countries. In 2005, Padilla and two other defendants were charged with operating a cell that supported Islamic terrorist groups in Eastern Europe. Terrorist cells are groups

What Is a Dirty Bomb?

A dirty bomb may contain radioactive material, but it is not regarded as a nuclear weapon. In the United States, nuclear weapons are guarded closely by the armed forces. Only twice in history have they been used—atomic bombs were detonated over the Japanese cities of Hiroshima and Nagasaki in 1945, bringing a swift end to World War II. More than 200,000 Japanese citizens were killed in the blasts.

A dirty bomb would be far less sophisticated and far less deadly. However, radioactive material is readily available in the United States in quantities large enough to pose a lethal risk. For example, hospitals use radioactive material to take X-rays and sterilize instruments. Food processing plants use radioactive waves to clean meat. And construction crews employ radioactive sensors to test welded seams.

Hospitals, meat processing plants, and construction sites are all likely to be less secure than a U.S. government weapons depot. Therefore, law enforcement officials are concerned that such locations could provide an ample supply of radioactive material to a terrorist.

that work either independently or together to carry out secret, often destructive, plots. The cell had been under FBI observation since the early 1990s. Federal intelligence agents had wiretapped phone conversations made by the three men. But the wall prevented the agents from using the information against the suspects in criminal court.

After the Patriot Act was signed into law, the FBI obtained new wiretap warrants from the Foreign Intelligence Surveillance Court against Padilla and the other suspects from his cell. The FBI was then able to use information gleaned through the wiretaps to bring charges in criminal court against the alleged conspirators—something they would not have been able to do without the Patriot Act provision. During Padilla's 2007 trial, prosecutors introduced the transcripts from 123 phone calls made by the suspects as evidence that they were raising money to support terrorist acts overseas. Padilla had visited an al-Qaeda training camp in Afghanistan and had intentions to explode a dirty bomb on U.S. soil.

Exposed through E-mail

Many argue that the Patriot Act gives federal agents too much authority to mine data from personal computers. And yet, by tracing the Internet habits and accessing the e-mail of Mohammed Junaid Babar, federal agents broke open a plot to commit terrorist acts in Great Britain.

Investigated under the Patriot Act, Babar was found to support terrorist activities in the United States and elsewhere by supplying military gear to al-Qaeda and setting up a training camp in Pakistan. Provisions of the Patriot Act permitted the FBI to obtain Babar's library records and track Internet usage. Agents determined that Babar had been contacting al-Qaeda leaders using a public access computer at the library. This information led to Babar's arrest. Babar pleaded guilty.

After his arrest, Babar proved to be a valuable asset to law enforcement. By questioning Babar, federal agents learned of his knowledge of an al-Qaeda plot to explode several bombs in London, England. With information from Babar, London authorities were able to thwart the plans and arrest the suspects. In 2007, Babar testified against five men in that plot, helping British prosecutors win convictions against all of the defendants.

Great Britain's Defense Secretary Geoff Hoon speaks next to a map
of al-Qaeda training camps.

FBI Director Robert Mueller delivers an address discussing the balance of national security and civil liberties.

LAW ENFORCEMENT
WITHOUT THE
PATRIOT ACT

ritics of the Patriot Act assert that law enforcement agencies would be able to expose terrorist plans without the use of the Patriot Act's provisions. They argue that police have had the authority for decades to search a suspect's home, wiretap communication devices, and obtain other records that could help convict a suspect or gain intelligence information.

Those agents, however, were required to obtain a warrant from a judge in order to use such investigatory tools. In obtaining the warrant, agents had to provide the judge sufficient reason to conduct a search, use a wiretap, or employ other methods. Critics argue that agents were less likely to overstep their authority since they were required to provide solid reasoning to a judge for any of their activities.

Georgetown University law professor David Cole believes that if the Patriot Act had been in place prior to September 11, 2001, it probably could not have prevented the terrorist attacks. What may have helped, he says, is better police work, more agents assigned to terrorist investigations, and better equipment placed at their disposal. "There is no basis to believe the Patriot Act would have changed things," Cole says. "The problem

**In the Words of
Benjamin Franklin**

Benjamin Franklin took part in writing the U.S. Constitution, which prohibits the search and seizure of evidence without warrants. Franklin warned against giving up this important right in the name of law enforcement. He said, "They that can give up essential liberty to obtain a little temporary safety deserve neither liberty nor safety."[1]

Outdated Computers

In 2004, an internal investigation conducted by the Justice Department found that an outdated FBI computer was responsible for the failure of a memo to circulate suggesting that al-Qaeda terrorists were taking flying classes at commercial aviation schools in the United States. In addition, the National Commission on Terrorist Attacks on the United States called the FBI's computer system "woefully inadequate."[3] Even if the Patriot Act had been in place prior to September 11, the FBI may have lacked the computer equipment to manage an effective investigation.

was not that there was any legal barrier that forbade investigation or follow-up. The problem was that there never was sufficient investigation. People didn't connect the dots—not because they couldn't, but because there were so many dots."[2]

Too Much Information

Critics of the Patriot Act also argue that it may be ineffective. The act gives the FBI vast powers to accumulate information—sometimes, too much information. In late 2003, federal agents developed intelligence suggesting that the city of Las Vegas, Nevada, may be the target of a terrorist attack. The FBI responded by issuing National Security Letters to dozens of hotels and casinos in Las Vegas. They also demanded records of phone calls, credit card use, bank accounts, and other personal information on more than 1 million tourists who were staying in the city at the time.

It was so much information that the FBI could not process it all.

Although recipients of National Security Letters are prohibited under law from telling others that they receive the letters, there were simply too many people served with the letters to keep the matter a secret. Within a week, the letters had become the talk of the Las Vegas casino community. Soon, a reporter for a Las Vegas newspaper learned that dozens of casino executives had received National Security Letters as part of a terror cell investigation. By early January of 2004, the FBI dropped the investigation. The bureau had spent weeks trying to

Plea Bargaining with Terrorists

Federal officials insist that the Patriot Act is effective in finding terrorists, even if the perpetrators ultimately receive minor sentences. Many terrorists plea-bargain after they are arrested. They provide agents with information about the activities of other terrorists in exchange for pleading guilty to lesser offenses. Plea bargaining with suspects in exchange for information is a tactic that has been employed by police and prosecutors for years.

Barry M. Sabin, chief of the counterterrorism section of the U.S. Justice Department, insisted that the Patriot Act has resulted in taking more than 400 terrorists out of circulation in the United States. "A person could not have been put on this list [of terrorists] if there was not a concern about national security, at least initially," said Sabin. "Are all these people an ongoing threat presently? Arguably not. ... We are not trying to overstate or understate what we're doing. You don't want to put language or a label on people that is inconsistent with what they have done."[4]

analyze too many records and pulling its resources away from other cases, while its top-secret plans were leaked to the press. As for Las Vegas, the city was not attacked.

Few Active Plots

President Bush's announcement that the Patriot Act had led to the arrests of more than 400 terror suspects prompted critics to examine those figures. In 2005, the *Washington Post* reported that of the 401 people Bush claimed were arrested under the Patriot Act, only 39 were convicted of crimes related to terrorism. Most of the others were convicted of minor crimes, such as misusing credit cards. Many were released after charges were dropped. The newspaper also reported that the average prison sentence for all defendants convicted under the Patriot Act was 11 months, while many others received just a few weeks in jail if they received any time at all. Most defendants have had no connection to terrorism.

A year after the *Washington Post* questioned the effectiveness of the Patriot Act, a study by Syracuse University suggested that in the five years since the 2001 attacks, the number of terrorism investigations actually receded. The study reported that in the first few months following the September 11 attacks, federal agents and prosecutors had made use of the Patriot Act to bring charges against hundreds of defendants. But by 2006, the study said, the number of people charged with terrorism-related offenses had declined to pre-2001 levels. Therefore, even with the Patriot Act at their disposal, federal agents and prosecutors were charging approximately the same number of people with terrorism-related offenses as they had been charging before the Patriot Act had been signed into law.

The numbers unearthed by the *Washington Post* and Syracuse University provided critics with ammunition to suggest that the Patriot Act is ineffective. Those opposed to the Patriot Act argue that the huge tangle of data plaguing the FBI agents dispatched to Las Vegas in 2003 would suggest that the Patriot Act is worse

Terrorism Statistics

A 2006 study by Syracuse University found prosecutors had actually lodged charges against 335 individuals.

Of that number, the Syracuse study found:

- 213 were convicted by trial or pleaded guilty.
- 123 were sentenced to prison while 90 received no jail time.
- Only six defendants received sentences of 20 years or more. Meanwhile, eight defendants received sentences of 5 to 20 years, 18 defendants received sentences of between one and five years, and 91 received sentences of less than one year.

than ineffective. They assert that the law has the potential for tying up agents in a mountain of data. Meanwhile, their talents could be used elsewhere in investigations that may provide more substantial results.

Critics argue that the Patriot Act often had little or nothing to do with some of the arrests of key individuals for terrorist activities. These critics assert that the Patriot Act further complicates the law. Many believe that law enforcement agencies should receive more funding, more training, and better leadership rather than use the Patriot Act. Retired U.S. Army Colonel David Hunt, who is acknowledged as one of the military's foremost experts on terrorism, said,

> When we're assessing the Patriot Act, we need to understand that we already have most of the laws we need to fight terrorism in the United States. The laws in this country when printed would fill up a football stadium. We need our laws simplified, not made more complicated. ... We also need to enforce our laws better. We need more training, more money for our police, and better leadership from the guys in charge.[5]

Las Vegas has been the suspected target of a terrorist attack.

Protestors in North Carolina gather during Attorney General John Ashcroft's visit defending the Patriot Act.

ARE CIVIL LIBERTIES COMPROMISED?

Under one of the Patriot Act's lesser-known provisions, a store owner must file a report with the FBI if a customer spends more than $10,000 in cash. Customer names are then turned over to an FBI database of suspected terrorists. Additionally, that big one-time cash

purchase could spark a more in-
depth FBI inquiry into a person's
background.

Money Trail

That provision of the Patriot
Act was designed to help the FBI
follow a terrorist's money trail.
International terrorist groups
such as al-Qaeda often provide
money to their members. To hide
the source of their cash, terrorists
will "launder" their money. They
will spend the cash on expensive
items in stores. They then resell
the items and use that cash to buy
weapons and plan their attacks.
By requiring stores to report large
cash purchases, the FBI can use the
Patriot Act to initiate surveillance
on big spenders.

Some people are concerned
about the creation of a government
database that contains the names
of innocent Americans. They are

Credit Cards and the Patriot Act

Under the Patriot Act, the
federal government sup-
plies banks and credit
card companies a list of
any suspected terrorists
or organizations believed
to be financing terrorism.
The banks and credit card
companies have the op-
tion of running the names
of new bank customers
and credit card applicants
against the list to determine if any of the suspects
seek to use their services.

The Patriot Act also
gives permission to sev-
eral federal agencies to
obtain information on a
suspect's financial history
from banks and credit
card companies. Under
the 1978 Right to Finan-
cial Privacy Act, only law
enforcement agencies
could obtain that infor-
mation. The Patriot Act
expands that capability to
other agencies, including
the CIA.

also concerned about making business owners participate in what is ordinarily a police function. Critics suggest this provision will create a climate of suspicion within the community. When a young couple spends a lot of wedding cash on new furniture, for example, will the furniture store clerk regard them as possible terrorists? James M. Rockett, a California attorney who represents banks in disputes with the government, said,

> You're trying to turn an untrained populace into the monitors of money laundering activity. If you want to stop this, it's going to be done with police work, not tracking consumers' buying habits.[1]

NATIONAL WARRANTS

To search a suspect's home, business, car, or other property,

Material Support and Cookie Sales

Under the Patriot Act, people who provide "material support" to terrorists can be charged as accomplices. In 2004, U.S. Judge Audrey B. Collins of California ruled that section of the law was too vague to be enforced. Collins suggested that most people would have no idea that the humanitarian group they are supporting may also have a terrorist side. The judge ruled that "a woman who buys cookies at a bake sale outside her grocery story to support displaced ... refugees to find new homes could be held liable" if the sale was sponsored by an organization that also supports terrorism.[2]

a federal agent must obtain a warrant. Prior to the Patriot Act, a local judge had to issue the warrant. According to the Sixth Amendment to the Constitution, criminals must be prosecuted in the jurisdiction where the crime was committed. Under the Constitution, a defendant has the right to have his or her case heard by a local judge in front of a local jury. Over the years, the courts have interpreted the Sixth Amendment to apply to all matters relating to the case—including the issuance of a search warrant. Therefore, under the interpretation of the law, local judges must approve warrants.

What Is Probable Cause?

A police officer pulls a car over to the side of the road. The driver has long hair, a scruffy beard, and is wearing a T-shirt displaying a marijuana leaf. Based on the driver's appearance, the police officer strongly suspects the car contains drugs. Can he search the car? The answer is no. Even though the officer does not like the looks of the driver, he has no reason to suspect the car contains drugs. He has no probable cause to search the vehicle.

The Fourth Amendment to the Constitution guards citizens against warrantless searches and seizures. In cases where the police officer suspects a crime is being committed, and the officer has no time to request a warrant in court, the officer is permitted to conduct a search without a warrant. In such cases, the law specifically requires the officer demonstrate "probable cause" before conducting a search.

What if the police officer detects the aroma of marijuana in the car? The smell of marijuana would provide the police officer with probable cause to believe the vehicle contains an illegal substance. The officer is then permitted to conduct a lawful search.

On the Lookout

The Treasury Department has prepared a list of "specially designated nationals"—people or groups it suspects of supporting terrorism. The list contains more than 5,000 names and can be viewed online.

Under the Patriot Act, business owners are prohibited from dealing with people or organizations on the list. Small business owners complain that it would take too long to cull through all the names when a customer is standing across the counter. "Imagine one person coming to cash a check and going through a list," said Sonia Cheema, owner of the Bin & Barrel Mini Mart in Fremont, California. "It's going to be a lot of work. I don't think it's worth it."[4]

In terrorism cases, the Patriot Act permits a federal judge to issue a warrant that can be served anywhere in the country. It means a judge in Massachusetts can approve the search of a suspect's home in California. Congress agreed to this provision because time is often a crucial factor. With this provision, if a federal agent in Massachusetts finds evidence suggesting a terror plot was about to occur in California, that agent would be able to obtain a warrant that could be quickly executed wherever needed. "Speed can help save lives," Deputy Attorney General James B. Comey told a Senate committee hearing on the Patriot Act in 2004.[3]

Civil libertarians question that logic. They contend that giving federal agents the right to obtain nationwide warrants enables them to go "forum shopping." They suggest that an agent will seek an area or state that is known to be lenient when it comes to issuing search warrants, rather than take a chance on appearing before a strange judge who may ask tougher questions about whether the search is justified.

POULTRY PLANT SEARCH

Just a few months after the September 11, 2001, attacks, a federal judge in Virginia issued a search warrant for a chicken processing plant in Georgia operated by Mar-Jac Poultry, Inc. In seeking the warrant, the federal agents alleged that the owners of the plant had made donations to an organization believed to be financing terrorism. The agents searched the plant and found no evidence and the Mar-Jac owners were never prosecuted.

The attorney for Mar-Jac, Buddy Parker, suggested that the agents sought the warrant in Virginia rather than in Georgia because a Georgia judge may have known more about the company and questioned the agents more closely. Parker stated,

What magistrate judge is going to sit up there (in Virginia)
less than six months after 9–11, and critically look to see

*whether or not there's probable cause? Why should she care
about some poultry factory in Georgia?*[5]

A POTENTIAL SOURCE OF PROFILING

Many feel that Muslims living in the United
States have been the individuals most affected by the
Patriot Act. Many Muslims are legal visitors from
Islamic countries who have been investigated under
the Patriot Act for what has been determined to
be innocent activity. The case of Sami Omar al-
Hussayen is one such investigation. Al-Hussayen, a
computer science student at the University of Idaho,
was arrested after his Internet habits were monitored
under the Patriot Act.

A Saudi citizen, al-Hussayen was a webmaster
for a number of Islamic sites. Some of those sites
urged friendly relations with the United States and
cooperation with American authorities. Other sites
preached jihad, the Arabic word for "holy war,"
against the United States. Al-Hussayen was arrested
and charged under the Patriot Act for supporting
terrorism. During his trial, al-Hussayen testified
that he does not support jihad against the United
States and had simply been providing his Web page

Thousands of Muslims pray in downtown Cleveland, Ohio.

expertise in order to gain experience as a Web designer. Although he realized the content on some of the pages was inflammatory and anti-American, al-Hussayen did not concern himself with the messages on the pages.

The government expected al-Hussayen to be convicted. Instead, the Idaho jury found him not guilty. After the trial, the jurors said that the government violated al-Hussayen's right to free speech. ⌐

Sami Omar al-Hussayen

*Senate Intelligence Committee Chairman Pat Roberts supports
the Patriot Act.*

ARE CIVIL LIBERTIES
PROTECTED?

*D*espite the issues raised by many
librarians, civil libertarians, and other
opponents of the Patriot Act, public opinion
polls have consistently shown that the majority of

Americans do not believe the law is intrusive or, if they do, they are willing to sacrifice some of their civil liberties to protect human life. The polls show that most Americans agree with U.S. Senator Pat Roberts of Kansas and other Patriot Act proponents who insist that alarmists have blown the privacy issues involved with the law out of proportion. Senator Roberts has argued that the FBI cannot fight terrorists without the Patriot Act.

FAVORABLE PUBLIC OPINION

In 2003, one of the first major polls commissioned on public opinion regarding the Patriot Act reported that 38 percent of Americans found the Patriot Act "just right," while 28 percent said it gave the U.S. government too much power. Another 12 percent of the respondents called for the Patriot Act to provide police with even more tools to uncover terrorists.

In 2006, Congress reauthorized most of the components of the Patriot Act. A few months later, another poll posed this question:

What do you think is more important right now—for the federal government to investigate possible terrorist threats, even if that intrudes on personal privacy; or for the federal

Expanding Existing Laws

Patriot Act supporter Mary Beth Buchanan, U.S. attorney for western Pennsylvania, questions how civil libertarians can oppose the law when most of the provisions of the Patriot Act have been on the books for years. According to Buchanan, the Patriot Act simply took existing laws and expanded them so they could be better used to find terrorists.

Buchanan said, "The Patriot Act contains 157 sections ... All but a handful of provisions are uncontroversial. Most of the act's sections are amendments to pre-existing laws. It is very difficult to form an opinion about the act just by simply reading it."[2]

government not to intrude on personal privacy, even if that limits its ability to investigate possible terrorist threats?[1]

Sixty-five percent of the respondents said it is permissible for the federal government to investigate terrorist attacks, even if it became necessary for federal agents to intrude on personal privacy. Less than half—32 percent—said they would prefer the government stay out of people's private lives, even if it hampered terrorism investigations.

Polls suggest that the majority of people are willing to cooperate in terror investigations. Many people realize that they could unknowingly have had contact with a terrorist. If they could help provide investigators with a lead by making their phone records or other information available, most people responded that they were willing to do what they can.

HARMLESS TO INNOCENT PEOPLE

Proponents also suggest that the information obtained under the Patriot Act is harmless to innocent people. After all, would most law-abiding people care if the FBI knows the titles of the books they check out of the library? Would that information really provide the government with information that it could later use against an innocent person?

In fact, the records of many libraries have been searched—often at the invitation of the librarians themselves. In Winslow Township, New Jersey, librarians at the South County Regional Library grew concerned about the frequent visits of a man who appeared to be of Middle Eastern ethnicity. Shortly after the terrorist attacks of 2001, librarians started noticing the man using the library's computer terminals virtually every day. At one point, a librarian noticed the man was studying a photograph of al-Qaeda leader Osama bin Laden on the computer screen. "This part of the county is a very rural area," said Claudia Sumler, director of the

Winslow Township library system. "He just looked different."[3]

So a librarian contacted the police, who initiated surveillance on the man. According to the police report, the man parked a car with Pennsylvania license plates every day in the library's parking lot, then spent hours at the computer terminals. He would take breaks to make frequent telephone calls at a pay phone. A police report stated,

> *He is on the computer for hours at a time and will go to the pay phone and be on it for at least two hours straight, and then use his cell phone for about a half-hour, then go back to the computer for hours.*[4]

The Winslow Township case occurred before Congress enacted the Patriot Act. Therefore, federal agents did not have access to National Security

Libraries Are Often Searched

According to statistics compiled by the American Library Association, between October 2001 and September 2005, 63 public libraries and 74 college campus libraries had turned over records to federal agents under the Patriot Act.

The American Library Association remains vehemently opposed to making library records available under the Patriot Act. In Guilford, Vermont, a sign posted in the public library reads:
"Q: How can you tell when the FBI has been to your library?
A: You can't."[5]

The privacy of library records and readership habits has caused much controversy in the Patriot Act debate.

Letters, which could have given them access to the man's library records quickly and without judicial oversight. Instead, the agents had to acquire a subpoena to find out what was going on at the South County Regional Library. A prosecutor appeared before a judge, who approved a subpoena to obtain the library's records. After the subpoena was served on the South County Regional Library, librarians turned over the records of the man's reading and Internet habits.

The FBI visited the mysterious man. It turned out that the library user, Charanjit Vedi, was not from a Middle East country but had moved to New Jersey from India to attend medical school. The reason his car displayed out-of-state license plates was because he had recently moved to New Jersey from Pennsylvania and had not yet obtained new plates. The South County Regional Library was, in fact, less than a mile from his new home.

Why had he been looking at a photo of bin Laden? It was a few days after the September 11 attacks and the medical student,

---

Law Too Complex to Understand?

Opponents of the Patriot Act maintain that the 342-page law is too complex for most people to understand. They suggest that if people truly took the time to read the Patriot Act and assessed how it has impacted civil liberties, they would be less likely to support the law.

Meanwhile, supporters of the Patriot Act insist that positive poll numbers do reflect strong support for the law. Justice Department spokesman Mark Corallo stated,

> There is a very, very small group of people who are criticizing the act, but they are actually getting about 95 percent of the media attention. We think the debate is healthy. We would just like the debate to be on balanced grounds. The average American certainly thinks that [the Bush] administration has been respectful of civil liberties.[6]

like millions of other people, was interested in learning about the mastermind of the terrorist attacks. Finding no reason to probe further, the FBI closed the investigation.

As for Vedi, he harbored no ill will toward the FBI or the librarians at the South County Regional Library. He said he understood the federal agents had to do their jobs and check out all leads—even if he did find himself at the center of the investigation. Vedi, who said he intends to pursue American citizenship, said, "I love this country."[7]

Elliot Turrini, a former federal prosecutor who helped draft the Patriot Act, said that while librarians may think they are protecting the rights of their members by guarding their privacy, they should not lose sight of the fact that it is far more important to protect the lives of their members. He said,

> You should be worried about your patrons' privacy, but you should also be worried about your patrons' well-being if the library is a place where the computer criminals can go without fear. If the library wants to serve its patrons, it must think about both sides of the issue. A knee-jerk reaction to protect privacy without a view of the total cost of your privacy policy is silly.[8]

TRUSTED TO RESPECT PRIVACY

Since the Patriot Act was enacted, federal officials have consistently said that they would not target innocent Americans and that they can be trusted to respect people's privacy. Assistant FBI Director Michael Mason stated,

> I don't necessarily want somebody knowing what videos I rent or the fact that I like cartoons. (But if those records) are never used against a person, if they're never used to put him in jail, or deprive him of a vote, then what is the argument?[9]

George W. Bush speaking in defense of the Patriot Act

The Federal Bureau of Investigation issues National Security Letters.

ABUSE OF THE
PATRIOT ACT

ven some of the Patriot Act's strongest supporters admit that there have been abuses. In March 2007, Glenn A. Fine, the inspector general for the Justice Department, issued a report detailing several instances in which the FBI issued National Security Letters improperly. According to Fine's report, some National Security Letters were issued without proper authorization, some were issued to people who had no connection to terrorist investigations, and some letters were issued for totally false purposes.

Fine's report examined 77 cases investigated by the FBI between 2003 and 2005. In examining these cases, a typical error cited by Fine was the demand for information from the wrong people due to typographical errors in the National Security Letters. In his report, Fine said he did not believe that federal agents had purposely violated the terms of the Patriot Act. Rather, his report suggested that FBI staff members were guilty of mismanagement, poor record keeping, and ignorance of their duties under the law.

For example, the report found that FBI agents did not accurately report the number of National Security Letters they issued. By law, the FBI must report to Congress the number of letters it has issued. But Fine's report found that the agency kept as many as 20 percent of the letters a secret—mostly due to clerical errors.

Reacting to the report, civil libertarians were not willing to attribute the mistakes to human error. They charged that the government's accumulation of data under the Patriot Act was operating without checks and balances. And for whatever reason, the records of innocent people had been harvested by an out-of-control law enforcement agency. "This confirms some of our worst suspicions," said Anthony D. Romero, executive director of the ACLU.[1]

Critics of the Patriot Act found that several members of Congress agreed with that position. U.S. Senator Arlen Specter of Pennsylvania said, "This is, regrettably, part of an ongoing process where the federal authorities are not really sensitive to privacy and go far beyond what we have authorized."[2]

Meeting in Secret

The Sixth Amendment to the Constitution guarantees the right to a public trial. However, certain courts, or cases, are permitted to be held privately. Proceedings of the Foreign Intelligence Surveillance Court are held in secret. It meets in a small, windowless room at the Justice Department headquarters in Washington, D.C. The court's location is not listed on the directory in the lobby. It has no listed phone number.

ILLEGAL WIRETAPS

Although Fine's report attributed the Patriot Act abuses mostly to administrative errors, other investigators found far more serious breaches of the law. In 2005, many newspapers revealed that federal agents had conducted a number of illegal wiretaps on phone calls made overseas by suspected terrorists. The wiretaps were initiated without warrants issued by the Foreign Intelligence Surveillance Court.

For the first 22 years of the court's operation, judges on the court found few reasons to question the purpose of the warrants—of more than 18,000 requests for warrants, almost none were turned down. Prior to the Patriot Act, the Foreign Intelligence Surveillance Court consisted of seven judges. With the Patriot Act, Congress recognized that the court's workload

Public Divided on Wiretapping

In February 2006, an Associated Press poll indicated 56 percent of the respondents believed federal agents should obtain a warrant before they initiate electronic surveillance, while 42 percent said it is permissible to wiretap without a warrant. The news service noted that support for warrantless wiretapping increased as President Bush traveled the nation speaking in favor of it.

was likely to increase. Therefore, four judges were added to the court.

After the enactment of the Patriot Act, the number of warrant requests did increase. In the four years following the September 11 attacks, there was an approximate 80 percent annual increase in the court's caseload. However, it became clear that the court started issuing warrants more carefully. In the years prior to the Patriot Act, virtually no warrants had been turned down.

The Brandon Mayfield Case

In May 2004, terrorists detonated bombs in Madrid, Spain, killing 191 people. During their investigation of the bombing, Madrid police found a fingerprint on a bag left behind by one of the terrorists. Assisting the Madrid police, the FBI compared the print to the millions of fingerprint records it has accumulated. Days after the bombing, the FBI arrested Brandon Mayfield, an Oregon lawyer.

Mayfield's fingerprint was on file because he had served in the U.S. Army. In investigating Mayfield, the FBI employed the Patriot Act to eavesdrop on his telephone conversations and perform a sneak-and-peek search of his home. During the investigation, the FBI learned that Mayfield had recently converted to Islam.

Three weeks after his arrest, Mayfield was released from jail. Madrid police, who performed their own fingerprint analysis, determined the print had not been left by Mayfield.

Mayfield sued the FBI, claiming the agency misused its powers under the Patriot Act to probe his background and that, after learning he converted to Islam, he was arrested mostly on that basis. In 2006, the FBI settled the lawsuit, agreeing to pay Mayfield $2 million to compensate him for his false imprisonment. Meanwhile, a second lawsuit filed by Mayfield, which seeks to have the Patriot Act declared unconstitutional, continues to make its way through the courts.

In the years following the Patriot Act, the court either rejected eavesdropping warrants or placed constraints on their use in nearly 180 cases.

Faced with constraints on investigations, the Bush administration authorized its agents to install the eavesdropping equipment without obtaining the warrants approved by the secret court. James Bamford, an authority on the Foreign Intelligence Surveillance Court, stated:

> They wanted to expand the number of people they were eavesdropping on, and they didn't think they could get the warrants they needed from the court to monitor these people. The ... court has shown its displeasure by tinkering with these applications by the Bush administration.[3]

In early 2007, faced with public uproar over the illegal wiretapping,

Judge James Robertson

U.S. Judge James Robertson, who resigned in protest from the Foreign Intelligence Surveillance Court, is no stranger to controversial decisions. In 2006, the judge ordered the federal government to redesign its paper currency, finding that printing all denominations in the same size presented a handicap to blind people. The government has appealed his decision.

Even after leaving the Foreign Intelligence Surveillance Court, Robertson remained a steadfast supporter of the court's mission. In testimony before Congress, he urged lawmakers to maintain the court's authority over electronic surveillance in national security cases.

Senator Patrick Leahy speaks in 2007 about warrantless wiretapping programs.

Bush administration officials acknowledged that they shut down the program. Investigators said that in the future, they would always seek authority for wiretaps from the special court. Still, subpoenas were issued to White House officials in search of answers. High-ranking members of the White House staff, the Justice Department, and other federal agencies found themselves answering to the courts for abuse of the Patriot Act.

JUSTICE DEPARTMENT PURGE

Early in 2007, the Justice Department dismissed eight U.S. attorneys. The attorneys oversaw the regional offices of the Justice Department that perform the investigations and prosecutions of people who violate federal crimes— including terrorists.

By law, prospective U.S. attorneys must undergo Senate confirmation, but that process can often take several months. Typically, the confirmation process involves an investigation into the background of the candidate, a probe into why the vacancy occurred, a hearing before the Senate Judiciary Committee, and a full vote scheduled on the Senate floor. The Bush administration felt that in times of crisis, an ongoing investigation could be compromised due to a vacancy in a U.S. attorney's position. In 2006, Congress

"At the Pleasure of the President"

Since the days of Andrew Jackson, presidents have maintained the right to hire and fire political appointees. U.S. attorneys fall into that category. It is not unusual for a new president to fire the entire staff of 93 federal prosecutors upon taking office—particularly if those attorneys were hired by a predecessor of a different political party.

During the controversy over the firings of the eight U.S. attorneys, White House Press Secretary Tony Snow insisted, during a media briefing, that President George W. Bush was within his rights to seek their dismissals. Snow said, "The most important principle here is people do serve at the pleasure of the president."[4]

inserted a provision in the Patriot Act that permitted the Bush administration to appoint temporary U.S. attorneys without Senate confirmation.

Some U.S. attorneys disagreed with this provision. Attorneys who resisted the pressure were fired and replaced with attorneys who were believed to be more willing to investigate members of the opposition party. Once the attorney vacancies were created, the Bush administration used the new Patriot Act provision to place other appointees. These people were able to take office without a Senate confirmation or an investigation into why the vacancy was made available in the first place. California Senator Dianne Feinstein stated,

> *For over 150 years, the process of appointing interim U.S. attorneys has worked with virtually no problems. Now, just one year after receiving unchecked authority in a little-known section added to the Patriot Act last spring, the administration has significantly abused its discretion.* [5]

Former Attorney General Alberto Gonzales during his swearing-in

Pro-Taliban supporters listen to an audiotaped speech during a rally near the Afghan border.

STILL SEEKING
SOLUTIONS

ollowing the attacks of September 11, 2001, terrorists struck in Great Britain, Spain, Russia, Jordan, and several other countries. The United States has been spared further attacks. Many people believe the Patriot Act is the reason.

"The Patriot Act has accomplished exactly what it was designed to do," President George W. Bush said in 2006. "It has helped us detect terrorist cells, disrupt terrorist plots and save American lives."[1]

The U.S. government has taken actions to diminish the threat of terrorism that have had nothing to do with the Patriot Act. Since the fall of 2001, U.S. troops have occupied Afghanistan, where they ousted the Taliban regime and helped install a democratic government. This new government will not harbor terrorists. Taliban guerillas remain a threat in Afghanistan, but it is unlikely that they will regain control of their nation's government.

HANDFUL OF CHANGES

When Congress originally passed the Patriot Act in the fall of 2001, lawmakers included a

The JFK Plot

When federal officials announced they had broken a terrorist plot to blow up the John F. Kennedy Airport in New York City, they described the massive devastation that would have occurred had the terrorists succeeded.

A closer look at the scheme revealed, however, that the suspects were penniless drifters who had no access to explosives and no expertise in using them. Michael Greenberger, director of the Center for Health and Homeland Security at the University of Maryland, said, "I think they were correct to take this seriously, but there's a pattern here of Justice Department attorneys overstating what they have. I think they feel under tremendous pressure to vindicate the elaborate counterterrorism structure they've created since 9/11, including the Patriot Act."[2]

"sunset" provision. This clause would have canceled the law unless lawmakers acted by the end of 2005 to reauthorize the measure. In late 2005, when it appeared that there was no consensus on renewing the Patriot Act, Congress voted to extend the act temporarily until the concerns of members were resolved. Finally, in March 2006, members of Congress worked out a compromise. With a handful of changes, the Patriot Act was reauthorized.

The measures that permit roving wiretaps and the seizure of private

Acts of Terrorism Since September 11, 2001

The United States has been spared a major terrorist attack since September 11, 2001, but other countries have been far less fortunate. Major acts of terrorism that have been committed include:

- Jordan, November 9, 2005: Three hotels in the capital city of Amman were bombed, taking the lives of 67 victims.
- Egypt, July 23, 2005: Bombs ignited in the Egyptian resort Sharm el Sheikh and killed more than 80 people, mostly foreign tourists.
- Great Britain, July 7, 2005: Suicide bombers targeted three subway trains and a bus in London, killing 56 people.
- Russia, September 1, 2004: A group of 30 armed men and women demanding independence for Chechnya seized a school in the city of Beslan, taking 1,100 hostages. After a day-long standoff, police staged a siege on the school; more than 300 children and adults died in the gunfire.
- Spain, March 11, 2004: Terrorists struck four commuter trains in Madrid, exploding bombs that killed 191 people.
- Indonesia, October 12, 2002: More than 200 people died in two bomb attacks on nightclubs on the island of Bali.

business records were extended only through 2009, when they will be reviewed again. Also, the Patriot Act's authority over National Security Letters was reined in somewhat. Recipients of the letters still cannot discuss them with other people, but they can now hire an attorney and challenge the letters in court. Essentially, Congress adopted as law the court order issued in the Connecticut library John Doe case.

Libraries were given some special protection in the new act. Under the amended law, federal agents now have to obtain a warrant or subpoena to access library records. In other words, they have to operate under the same rules for obtaining library records that were in effect before the enactment of the Patriot Act.

One major provision that had been challenged by privacy

New Rules for National Security Letters

In 2007, the FBI refined its internal guidelines that instruct agents how to obtain the National Security Letters in order to help curb abuses of the letters. Now, the agents must be very specific in detailing the exact information they are requesting. That will help prevent massive data sweeps that could scoop up personal information on innocent people that is of no use to the investigation.

Also, the new guidelines prevent agents from entering the data they accumulate into FBI computers until they first verify that the information is vital to investigations.

advocates is the permission granted to federal agents to conduct sneak-and-peek searches. Congress permitted the sneak-and-peek searches to continue. But now the subjects of the searches must be notified within 30 days of the search. The search no longer can remain a secret indefinitely.

Spies on Campus

The FBI believes terror suspects have turned to college campuses in search of information they can use to develop weapons. According to the FBI, college campuses are open environments where security is often neglected. In 2007, the Boston field office of the FBI warned officials at Harvard University, Massachusetts Institute of Technology, and the University of Massachusetts to be wary of "students" who may show an unusual amount of interest in sensitive research. The agency plans to contact all colleges in the United States.

FUTURE CHANGES AHEAD

Based on abuses of the Patriot Act revealed in 2006 and 2007, Congress initiated probes of the warrantless wiretapping by the Bush administration as well as the political firings of the eight federal prosecutors. In the meantime, Congress took steps to ensure that the Patriot Act would not be used again to further a political agenda. In May 2007, lawmakers repealed the portion of the Patriot Act providing for the appointment of U.S. attorneys without Senate confirmation.

Civil libertarians and some members of Congress want to

see further amendments to the law. Soon after the Patriot Act was reauthorized, Senator Arlen Specter introduced Senate Bill 2369, which privacy advocates have endorsed. Under Specter's amendments, the FBI would have to show a direct connection between terrorism and the suspect in question before it could seize business records. This provision would, for example, protect innocent people making large cash purchases from being swept up in a terrorism investigation. Specter also proposed stricter rules on sneak-and-peek searches, requiring suspects to be notified within seven days of the searches.

While Congress and the president regard the Patriot Act as a valuable antiterrorism tool, lawmakers still believe it is important to monitor how federal agents use the law. When the

New Data Mining Computer

Federal agencies have collected millions of pieces of information on Americans; soon, they hope to have a new supercomputer that will help analyze the data. The project to build the massive computer is known as Analysis, Dissemination, Visualization, Insight, and Semantic Enhancement, or ADVISE.

The computer is designed to analyze the habits of people to determine whether they fit the profile of a terrorist. Jeffrey Ullman, computer science professor at Stanford University in California, said, "If a computer suspects me of being a terrorist, but just says maybe an analyst should look at it. ... Well, that's no big deal. This is the type of thing we need to be willing to do, to give up a certain amount of privacy."[3]

reauthorized Patriot Act came before the U.S. House in 2006, it barely passed.

The record shows that the Patriot Act has been effective and that the FBI has been able to use it to thwart terrorists such as Mohammed Junaid Babar. But the record also shows that the law has been abused—often involving well-meaning immigrants, such as in the case of Sami Omar al-Hussayen. While many support the law and believe it provides important tools for uncovering terror plots, many others believe that provisions within the Patriot Act put civil liberties at a great risk. Ultimately, however, in the heated debate over national security and privacy rights, U.S. citizens will decide their own fates through their elected lawmakers and the power of voting. ⌐

The Capitol building in Washington, D.C., where lawmakers will decide
the fate of the Patriot Act

TIMELINE

1861	1918	1919
On April 27, President Abraham Lincoln suspends habeas corpus to help protect the Union from Southern spies.	Congress passes the Sedition Act, making it illegal to criticize the U.S. government.	U.S. Attorney General A. Mitchell Palmer uses the Sedition Act to deport some foreign-born communists and anarchists.

1947	1971	1974
The House Un-American Activities Committee (HUAC), convenes its first hearings to investigate the influence of communists.	COINTELPRO, the FBI's secret program of domestic spying, is shut down after newspapers report its existence.	Congress enacts the Privacy Act on December 31.

1921	1940	1942
Reacting to the abuses of the Palmer Raids, Congress repeals the Sedition Act.	Congress passes the Smith Act, making it illegal to advocate the overthrow of the U.S. government.	On February 19, President Franklin D. Roosevelt orders 110,000 Japanese Americans held in internment camps during World War II.

1978	2001	2001
Congress creates the Foreign Intelligence Surveillance Court to enable intelligence agents to monitor the activities of suspected spies.	On September 11, airliners hijacked by terrorists kill more than 3,000 people.	On October 26, President Bush signs the USA Patriot Act, giving federal agents vast authority to gather data as they pursue terrorists.

TIMELINE

2001

On December 22, Richard Reid is overpowered by passengers aboard a transatlantic flight as he tries to ignite a shoe bomb.

2002

On April 30, Mohamed Hussein becomes the first defendant convicted under the Patriot Act.

2002

On May 8, José Padilla is arrested on suspicion that he planned to detonate a dirty bomb in the United States.

2005

On June 12, the *Washington Post* reports that of the 401 people arrested under the Patriot Act, just 39 were convicted of terrorism crimes.

2005

U.S. District Court Judge Janet C. Hall rules that recipients of National Security Letters have the right to contest the letters in court.

2005

On December 16, the Bush administration acknowledges that it has conducted illegal wiretaps on terrorism suspects.

2003	2003	2004
Numerous city and state legislatures pass resolutions calling for Congress to repeal or alter the Patriot Act.	In December, FBI agents investigating a terrorist threat in Las Vegas, Nevada, find themselves overwhelmed by information.	On June 10, University of Idaho student Sami Omar al-Hussayen is acquitted of charges of providing support to Islamic terrorist groups.

2006	2007
On March 9, President Bush reauthorizes the Patriot Act, with changes to reduce the government's access to private records.	Congress investigates the use of the Patriot Act to fire eight federal prosecutors, allegedly for political purposes.

ESSENTIAL FACTS

AT ISSUE

The Patriot Act enabled federal agents to obtain National Security Letters to collect evidence in criminal cases. Prior to the Patriot Act, the letters could be used only for collection of intelligence. The Patriot Act empowered federal agents to obtain warrants from the Foreign Intelligence Surveillance Court to wiretap individuals suspected of criminal activity. Prior to the Patriot Act, the court issued wiretap warrants strictly for intelligence-gathering purposes.

Opposed

❖ The Patriot Act enables federal agents to accumulate data on innocent citizens.

❖ The Patriot Act is ineffective because it often causes federal law enforcement agencies to be swamped with too much information.

❖ The Patriot Act does not ensure proper judicial oversight over evidence-gathering procedures.

❖ Sneak-and-peek searches may violate the Fourth Amendment guarantee against warrantless searches and seizures.

❖ The Patriot Act gives federal agents the right to investigate the reading habits of Americans.

In Favor

❖ No terrorist attack has been committed in the United States since the passage of the Patriot Act.

❖ The Patriot Act enables federal agencies to share information.

❖ The Patriot Act has been employed to thwart common criminals, such as Internet predators and drug dealers.

❖ Under the Patriot Act, federal agents can act quickly against a terrorist threat by obtaining warrants that can be served nationally.

❖ The Patriot Act enables federal agents to locate sources of money that are used to finance terrorist cells.

CRITICAL DATES

September 11, 2001
Islamic terrorists killed more than 3,000 people by hijacking four airliners and crashing them in New York City, Washington, D.C., and western Pennsylvania.

October 26, 2001
The original version of the Patriot Act was signed into law by President George W. Bush; the act passed in Congress by an overwhelming margin in both houses and after little debate.

September 9, 2005
A federal judge overturned the portion of the Patriot Act that prevents librarians and other recipients of National Security Letters from challenging them in court.

March 9, 2006
Reauthorization of the Patriot Act was signed into law by President George W. Bush.

QUOTES

"The Patriot Act has accomplished exactly what it was designed to do. It has helped us detect terrorist cells, disrupt terrorist plots and save American lives."—*President George W. Bush*

"Were a totalitarian government to be imposed on us, its inception would look strikingly like these provisions. History teaches us that such evils almost always begin justified by concerns for public safety and amid general panic. Without judicial safeguards, federal agents could abuse their newly authorized tools in situations neither Congress nor the American people contemplated."—*John A. Russo, director of the National League of Cities*

ADDITIONAL RESOURCES

SELECT BIBLIOGRAPHY

Burroughs, Todd Steven. "The ACLU on Preserving Civil Liberties." *New Crisis*. Nov.-Dec. 2001.

Coll, Steve. "The Unthinkable." *New Yorker*. 12 Mar. 2007.

Conan, Neal. "Analysis: New Anti-Terrorism Bill." *Talk of the Nation*. National Public Radio Talk. 30 Oct. 2001.

Eggen, Dan, and Julie Tate. "U.S. Campaign Produces Few Convictions on Terrorism Charges." *Washington Post*. 12 June 2005.

Farmer, John, Jr., "At Freedom's Edge: Liberty, Security and the Patriot Act." *Newark Star-Ledger*. 3 July 2005 <http://www.nj.com/news/ledger/index.ssf?/news/ledger/stories/patriotact/partone.html>.

Gellman, Barton. "The FBI's Secret Scrutiny: In Hunt for Terrorists, Bureau Examines Records of Ordinary Americans." *Washington Post*. 6 Nov. 2005.

Hunt, David. *They Just Don't Get It: How Washington is Still Compromising Your Safety—And What You Can Do About It*. New York: Crown Forum, 2005.

FURTHER READING

Johnson, Terry. *Legal Rights*. New York: Facts on File, 2005.

Miller, Debra. *The Patriot Act*. Farmington Hills, MI: Lucent Books, 2007.

Torr, James D. *Civil Liberties and the War on Terrorism*. San Diego: Lucent Books, 2004.

Web Links

To learn more about privacy rights and the Patriot Act, visit ABDO Publishing Company on the World Wide Web at **www. abdopublishing.com**. Web sites about privacy rights and the Patriot Act are featured on our Book Links page. These links are routinely monitored and updated to provide the most current information available.

For More Information

National Constitution Center
Independence Mall, 525 Arch Street, Philadelphia, PA 19106
215-409-6600
www.constitutioncenter.org
The museum dedicated to the history of the U.S. Constitution and its application to American society features many interactive exhibits that help explain the Constitution's provisions, including the guarantee of due process and the prohibition on warrantless searches and seizures.

Supreme Court of the United States
1 First Street Northeast, Washington, DC 20543
202-479-3211
www.supremecourtus.gov
The U.S. Supreme Court hears many cases to determine the constitutionality of issues in American life. The court's sessions are open to the public. Most arguments are heard 10:00-11:00 a.m. Mondays, Tuesdays, and Wednesdays from October through April.

World Trade Center Memorial and Museum
One Liberty Plaza, New York, NY 10006
212-227-7722
www.buildthememorial.org
Scheduled for opening in 2009, the facility in Lower Manhattan will be dedicated to the event that prompted the Patriot Act—the September 11, 2001, terrorist attacks.

Glossary

Afghanistan
> The war-torn Islamic nation in central Asia where the terrorism-supporting government known as the Taliban rose to power in the 1990s.

al-Qaeda
> The international terrorist organization responsible for planning and executing the September 11, 2001, attacks on the World Trade Center and the Pentagon; in Arabic, the term means "the base."

civil disobedience
> Actions such as trespassing and minor vandalism, illegal but usually nonviolent, in which activists hope to make political statements.

civil liberties
> The basic rights guaranteed to U.S. citizens by law.

communists
> Political activists who seek a society based on collective ownership of property; under communism, wealth is spread evenly among all citizens.

conservative
> A political movement whose members are wary of change and reform; in the United States, Republicans generally are regarded as conservatives.

data mining
> Examining large databases and other information centers in order to find new information.

Islamic fundamentalists
> Muslims who practice a form of Islam based on a literal interpretation of the Qur'an.

jihad
> An Arabic word that means "holy struggle;" some Islamic fundamentalists believe jihad requires them to eliminate, usually through violent means, nonbelievers of Islam.

liberal
> A political movement whose adherents readily accept change and reform; in American politics, Democrats are often regarded as more liberal than Republicans.

probable cause
> Evidence of a crime that permits a police officer to search property or make an arrest.

prosecutor
> A court official responsible for presenting evidence proving the guilt of a defendant.

Qur'an
> The sacred scriptures of the Islamic religion containing revelations made to the Prophet Muhammad by Allah.

subpoena
> A court order, issued by a judge or attorney, requiring a person to produce evidence or testify in court.

Taliban
> In Pashto, a language spoken in Afghanistan, the term means "students;" members of the Taliban are Islamic fundamentalists who controlled the Afghanistan government until they were deposed in 2001 by U.S. troops for harboring al-Qaeda.

terrorist
> An activist who employs violent acts to make a political statement.

warrant
> A court order issued by a judge giving permission to law enforcement officers to search private property or to perform other tasks to prevent or solve a crime.

wiretap
> An electronic device that enables law enforcement officers to listen to private telephone conversations.

Source Notes

Chapter 1. The Case of John Doe

1. Bob Kemper and Jeff Zeleny. "President Signs Bill Widening Powers for Police." *Chicago Tribune*. 27 Oct. 2001. A-1.

2. Russell Feingold. "A U.S. Senator Opposes the Patriot Act." address to the U.S. Senate, Washington, D.C., 25 Oct. 2001, reprinted in Louise I. Gerdes, ed. *The Patriot Act: Opposing Viewpoints*. Farmington Hills, MI: Greenhaven Press, 2005. 178.

3. John A. Russo. "Barriers to the Constitutional Right to Privacy: Patriot Act—Forgoing Liberty for Safety?" *San Francisco Chronicle*, 29 Jan. 2004. A-23.

4. Barton Gellman. "Court Vacates FBI Gag Order." *Washington Post*. 10 Sept. 2005. A-8.

5. George Christian. transcript of testimony submitted to the Senate Judiciary Subcommittee on the Constitution, Civil Rights and Property Rights, 11 Apr. 2007 <http://blogs.ala.org/oifphp?title=usapatriotact_nsl&more=1&c=1&tb=1&pb=1>.

6. Anthony York. "Ashcroft Eases Domestic Spy Rules." Salon.com. 31 May 2002. <http://dir.salon.com/story/politicsfeature/2002/05/31/fbi/index.html>.

Chapter 2. Swift Response to a Crisis

1. David Cole. "Enemy Aliens." 2003. 26 Sept. 2007 <http://www.law.georgetown.edu/alumni/publications/2003/magazineenemyaliens.html>.

2. Kim Zetter. "The Patriot Act is Your Friend." 24 Feb. 2004. 16 Nov. 2007 <http://www.wired.com/politics/law/news/2004/02/62388?currentpage=2>.

3. David Cole. "Enemy Aliens." 2003. 26 Sept. 2007 <http://www.law.georgetown.edu/alumni/publications/2003/magazineenemyaliens.html>.

4. George W. Bush. "Remarks on Signing the USA Patriot Act of 2001." Weekly Compilation of Presidential Documents. 29 Oct. 2001.

5. Todd Steven Burroughs, "The ACLU on Preserving Civil Liberties." *New Crisis*. Nov.-Dec. 2001. 13.

Chapter 3. Two Sides of the Debate

1. "A Resolution of the City Council of the City of North Pole Affirming Civil Rights and Liberties; Requesting Immediate Review

of Federal Measures that Infringe on Civil Liberties." 21 Apr. 2003. Bill of Rights Defense Committee. <http://www.bordc.org/detail.php?id=107>.

2. Mary Jo Patterson. "Changes in the Law Put Spotlight on a Shadowy Court." *Newark Star-Ledger*. 21 Aug. 2005. <http:/www.nj.com/news/ledger/index.ssf?/news/ledger/stories/patriotact partfive.html>.

3. George W. Bush. "Remarks on Signing the USA Patriot Act of 2001." Weekly Compilation of Presidential Documents. 29 Oct. 2001.

4. Kevin Coughlin. "Federal Investigators Can Listen, But Can They Hear?" *Newark Star-Ledger*. 28 Sept. 2005. <http://www.nj.com/news/ledger/index.ssf?/news/ledger/stories/patriotact partnine.html>.

Chapter 4. How the Patriot Act Benefits Law Enforcement

1. Sheryl Gay Stolberg. "Senate Passes Legislation to Renew Patriot Act." *New York Times*. 3 Mar. 2006. A-14.

2. George W. Bush. "The Patriot Act Should be Expanded." address before the Pennsylvania State Association of Township Supervisors, Hershey, PA, 19 Apr. 2004, reprinted in Louise I. Gerdes, ed. *The Patriot Act: Opposing Viewpoints*. Farmington Hills, MI: Greenhaven Press, 2005. 132.

Chapter 5. Law Enforcement without the Patriot Act

1. John Farmer Jr. "At Freedom's Edge: Liberty, Security and the Patriot Act." *Newark Star-Ledger*. 3 July 2005. <http://www.nj.com/news/ledger/index.ssf?/news/ledger/stories/patriotact/partone.html>.

2. Ibid.

3. Kevin Coughlin. "Federal Investigators Can Listen, But Can They Hear?" *Newark Star-Ledger*. 28 Sept. 2005. <http://www.nj.com/news/ledger/index.ssf?/news/ledger/stories/patriotact partnine.html>.

4. Dan Eggen and Julie Tate. "U.S. Campaign Produces Few Convictions on Terrorism Charges." *Washington Post*. 12 June 2005. A-1.

Source Notes Continued

5. David Hunt. *They Just Don't Get It: How Washington is Still Compromising Your Safety—And What You Can Do About It*. New York: Crown Forum, 2005. 169.

Chapter 6. Are Civil Liberties Compromised?
1. Scott Bernard Nelson. "New Federal Patriot Act Turns Retailers into Spies Against Customers." *Boston Globe*. 18 Nov. 2001.
2. Timothy Egan. "Computer Student on Trial Over Muslim Web Site Work." *New York Times*. 27 Apr. 2004. A-16.
3. John P. Martin. "Threat at a Casino Tests the Expanded Powers of Secrecy." *Newark Star-Ledger*. 28 Aug. 2005. <http://www. nj.com/news/ledger/index.ssf?/news/ledger/stories/patriotact/ partsix.html>.
4. Steve Johnson. "Money-Laundering Rules 'A Lot of Work'." *Honolulu Advertiser*. 29 Dec. 2004. <http://the.honoluluadvertiser. com/article/2004/Dec/29/bz/bz16p.html>.
5. John P. Martin. "Threat at a Casino Tests the Expanded Powers of Secrecy." *Newark Star-Ledger*. 28 Aug. 2005. <http://www. nj.com/news/ledger/index.ssf?/news/ledger/stories/patriotact/ partsix.html>.

Chapter 7. Are Civil Liberties Protected?
1. ABC News Poll, 5-7 Sept. 2006. <http://www.pollingreport. com/terror.htm>.
2. Mary Beth Buchanan. "Liberty and Security for All: The Balancing Act." *Pittsburgh Post-Gazette*. 21 Sept. 2003. < http://www. post-gazette.com/forum/comm/20030921edbuch0921p4.asp>.
3. Christine V. Baird. "Even the Libraries Can't Escape Expanded Powers to Spy." *Newark Star-Ledger*. 11 Sept. 2005. <http://www. nj.com/news/ledger/index.ssf?/news/ledger/stories/patriotact/ partseven.html>.
4. Ibid.
5. Ibid.
6. Peter Brownfield. "Patriot Act Opponents Say Law Endangers Rights." *Fox News*. 11 Sept. 2003 <http://www.foxnews.com/ story/0,2933,97003,00.html>.

7. Christine V. Baird. "Even the Libraries Can't Escape Expanded Powers to Spy." *Newark Star-Ledger*. 11 Sept. 2005. <http://www.nj.com/news/ledger/index.ssf?/news/ledger/stories/patriotact/partseven.html>.

8. Ibid.

9. Barton Gellman. "The FBI's Secret Scrutiny: In Hunt for Terrorists, Bureau Examines Records of Ordinary Americans."

Chapter 8. Abuse of the Patriot Act

1. David Stout. "FBI Head Admits Mistakes in Use of Security Act." *New York Times*. 10 Mar. 2007. A-1.

2. Ibid.

3. Stewart M. Powell. "Secret Court Modified Wiretap Requests." *Seattle Post-Intelligencer*. 24 Dec. 2005. <http://seattlepi.nwsource.com/national/253334_nsaspying24.html>.

4. Press Briefing by Tony Snow, White House news release, 16 Mar. 2007 <http://www.whitehouse.gov/news/releases/2007/03/20070316 4.html>.

5. Gail Russell Chaddock. "Eight Lost Their Jobs, Leading Democratic Lawmakers Try to Rein in Presidential Powers." *Christian Science Monitor*. 8 Mar. 2007 <http://www.csmonitor.com/2007/0308/p01s01-uspo.html>.

Chapter 9. Still Seeking Solutions

1. Nedra Pickler. "Bush Signs Renewal of Patriot Act into Law: Key Provisions were to Expire Today." *Bergen County Record*, 10 Mar. 2006. A-14.

2. Carol Eisenberg. "JFK Terror Plot: Credibility of Case in Question." *Newsday*. 6 June 2007 < http://www.newsday.com/news/nationworld/nation/ny-ushype065244078jun06,0,4911904.story?coll=ny-nationalnews-print>.

3. Mark Clayton. "U.S. Plans Massive Data Sweep." *Christian Science Monitor*. 9 Feb. 2006. <http://www.csmonitor.com/2006/0209/p01s02-uspo.html>.

INDEX

ABOUT THE AUTHOR

Hal Marcovitz is a former newspaper reporter who has written more than 100 books for young readers. In 2005, *Nancy Pelosi*, his biography of House Speaker Nancy Pelosi, was named to *Booklist* magazine's list of recommended feminist books for young readers. As a journalist, he has won three Keystone Press Awards, the highest award for newspaper reporting presented by the Pennsylvania Newspaper Association. He lives in Chalfont, Pennsylvania, with his wife and two daughters.

PHOTO CREDITS

Charles Dharapak/AP Images, cover, 3; Roberto Borea/AP Images, 6, 97; Shiho Fukada/AP Images, 12; Doug Mills/AP Images, 17, 18; Rhoda Baer, Georgetown University Law School/AP Images, 21; Ted S. Warren/AP Images, 27; Jeff Roberson/AP Images, 28; Susan Walsh/AP Images, 39, 84, 99; Kiichiro Sato/AP Images, 40, 98 (bottom); Alan Diaz/AP Images, 45, 98 (top); Reuters/Corbis, 49; Charles Krupa/AP Images, 50; Jae C. Hong/AP Images, 57; Karl DeBlaker/AP Images, 58; The Plain Dealer, Eustacio Humphrey/AP Images, 65; Moscow Pullman Daily News/AP Images, 67; Lauren Victoria Burke/AP Images, 68; Lisa Poole/AP Images, 73; David Duprey/AP Images, 77; Michael Sohn/AP Images, 78, 96 (bottom); Christopher Morris VII/AP Images, 87; AP Images, 88; Jupiterimages/AP Images, 95, 96 (top)

—